CLB 1946
© 1987 Illustrations and text: Colour Library Books Ltd,
    Guildford, Surrey, England.
Printed and bound in Barcelona, Spain by Cronion, S.A.
1987 edition published by Crescent Books, distributed by Crown Publishers, Inc.
ISBN 0 517 639505
h g f e d c b a

IRELAND

Designed and Produced by

Ted Smart & David Gibbon

CRESCENT BOOKS
NEW YORK

OVER the years the land of Ireland has become familiar to people throughout the world who have never visited the "Emerald Isle". It has featured in dozens of feature films and documentaries and was seen by many millions during the televising of Pope John Paul II's highly successful visit in September 1979.

What viewers throughout the world shared on their television screens was the rejoicing of a majority of a disciplined people, and a glimpse was caught of a land of much colour and contrast. The autumn sun shone, and a large fragment of the whole that goes to make up the Irish was witnessed by the viewing world. Although small in geographical and physical terms, this tiny spot on the globe gets its fair share of exposure on television, in the world's press, and on radio. More often than not its current news in relation to one area of the country is sad and violent and bloody, but at all times this small off-shore island of a slightly larger European off-shore island, commands the attention and interest of its many, many millions of relations throughout the world, and notably in Great Britain, in the United States, in Australia, and particularly in emergent African nations where Irish missionaries have laboured and taught for over a century.

There are, for example, one million Irish-born and over three million Irish-related people resident in Great Britain today, in fact, more Irish than there are living in Ireland, and between twenty and thirty millions more Irish born and Irish-related in America.

Not all of them know all that much about the country of their ancestors and its roots, and for those with a general interest in the Irish nation, some gathering of the facts, and a bird's-eye view, can help to broaden and deepen the interest in a place and a people which alternatively delights and exasperates the civilised world, but never loses its touch for the romantic or the magical, or its sense of humour or its sense of the absurd, and always remains supremely beautiful, and full of colour.

The island of Ireland is, of course, part of the main continent of Europe. It is situated as part of the most north-westerly area of the European land mass between fifty-one and a half degrees and fifty-five and a half degrees latitude north, and five and a half and ten and a half degrees longitude west.

Separating Ireland from Great Britain is the Irish Sea, about ten miles at its narrowest, and one hundred and twenty miles at its widest. The land of Ireland comprises 32,595 square miles, and roughly speaking, the greatest length of the country is three hundred and two miles, and at its greatest width it is one hundred and seventy-five miles. No point within the island is more than seventy or eighty miles from the sea-shore.

The Irish Sea to the east is about two hundred metres deep, and is a rough enough sea in the winter, particularly in the more exposed and open south-west. The Atlantic Ocean to the west presents an awesome sight at any time of the year, with its sixty foot rollers and breakers hurling themselves all down the west coast. America is two thousand four hundred miles away to the west.

The entire Irish coastline adds up to over three thousand five hundred miles.

Because of its sea-girt nature the land of Ireland enjoys a moderate climate. Winters are relatively mild, and summers reasonably warm, the occasional summer being positively Mediterranean. The months of July and August are the warmest, averaging 15°C or 59°F. May and June are the months with the most sun. Snow and ice, except on high mountains, are rare, but there is always the unexpected and an exceptional winter.

Overall, the moderate influence of the warm Gulf Stream, drifting down the west coast, makes for sub-tropical and unusual foliage and flowers and fauna in the south west.

From the prevailing winds coming in from the Atlantic Ocean comes the rain, which is heavier in the west, and averages about thirty inches in the east.

Because of its westerly geographical position, there are more hours of daylight in Ireland than in the rest of Europe and a clear sky with light and lucidity which is forever changing, and best described in paintings or visual terms as an "Expressionist" light. This is the overriding beauty above the landscape. To add to this overall beauty of sky and light, the physical features of Ireland are such that every range of scenery in Europe is available in one small isle. No two county divisions of the country are alike.

Generally speaking, Ireland comprises a central undulating plain of limestone, encircled by a coastal range of highland mountains of all sorts of geological structures and ages. The central plain is mostly bogland, with glacial deposits of clay and of sand, and scarred by hundreds of lakes. Scenically, Ireland is allied to Scotland and to Wales, but lost out, for good or evil, on coalfields.

With over eight hundred lakes and rivers, the land is well watered and beautified. The Shannon River is the longest, at 230 miles, and drains one-fifth of the whole of Ireland. A birds-eye view of the topography shows the Shannon flowing from north to south, through Lough Allen, Lough Ree and Lough Derg. To the west are Loughs Mask and Corrib. North of the Shannon source lie the Lower and Upper Lough Erne. Lough Neagh dominates the north-eastern corner with its Bann and Lagan rivers. The Boyne and the Liffey flow east-west. The Slaney, Barrow, Nore and Suir flow to the south-east, the Blackwater and Lee flow from the west to turn to the south. Lough Leane peeps out from the deep south-western corner.

Carrantuohill is the highest mountain peak in the

country at 3,414 feet, while Lough Neagh is the largest lake, at 153 square miles.

The south and south-westerly regions have areas of old red sandstone rocks with valleys of limestone. The west features limestone deserts, plus a mixture of granite, quartzite and igneous rocks. This is repeated in the north-east, where great basalt plateaux appear with the addition of granite mountains. Granite reappears in the east coast.

Twice Ireland was subjected to ice ages of glaciation, the first covering the entire country, the second extending to two-thirds of the country. The retreat of the glaciers has given ice-smoothed rocks, and glacial deposits of clay and gravel, providing a distinct character to the landscape.

Because of Ireland's position in Europe as the last country to suffer the last ice age, much of the earlier fauna and flora disappeared, and consequently there is much less in Ireland than in Britain, but it is also somewhat different, as Cantabrian plants, such as are found in Spain, are also found in Ireland, and even some North American types. Snakes, moles and weasels are not found in Ireland, as they are in England, and fewer types of mice. The Irish hare is nothing like the English hare, but has more in common with the Scottish hare. It is unusually large.

One area in the west of Ireland has rare alpine Arctic species of wild flowers, and the south-west flora is rich in Mediterranean species.

The bird life of Ireland is also rich, there being 380 species of wild birds, of which over 130 breed in the country. Three-quarters of the world's Greenland white-fronted geese spend their winters in Ireland, and the Atlantic coast gives safe harbour to most of the world's gannets and stormy petrels.

From the geographical location, its climate, its geological structure, its flora and fauna, emerges what might best be described as the anatomy of the landscape, so characteristic of Ireland, so different from, for example, that of England, which makes for an Irish scenery unaffected by an Industrial Revolution, which in turn has shaped the environment which produced its effects on the people who came to inhabit this off-shore island. This least populated country in Europe has today a population of approximately 4,700,000. They are, in the main, what might be best described as white Europeans, of many racial mixtures, the majority of whom, for historical reasons, could be described as Nordic. Being Irish, they have, of course, to be paradoxically different; so many brown-haired people have blue eyes, and many fair-haired people have brown eyes, and about one in twenty is a red-head.

It is impossible to say precisely when the first people came to the island of Ireland, or from whence they originally came. But concerning the earliest inhabitants, occasionally one comes across a historical quotation which is particularly apt and timeless. Concerning the early Celts, the Roman historian, Diodorus Siculus, who was a contemporary of Julius Caesar, made one very discerning statement. He wrote some forty books of history in Rome, of which some fourteen survive, and while he is not thoroughly reliable, he wrote of the Celts as follows:-

"Physically the Celts are terrifying in appearance, with deep-sounding and very harsh voices. In conversation they use few words and speak in riddles, for the greater part hinting at things and leaving a great deal to be understood. They frequently exaggerate in order to promote themselves at the expense of others. They are boasters and threateners, and given to boastful self dramatization, and yet they are quick of mind with good natural ability for learning."

Diodorus Siculus goes on to say that the Celts have bards or poets, who sometimes indulge in satire, and sometimes in praise.

From this comparatively early, but Roman quotation, it would seem that the early Celts had much in common with their ancestors of today; the Irish people, who still speak in riddles.

When it comes to the history of the Celtic peoples, and the earliest inhabitants of Ireland, you pay your money to the history experts, and take your choice. Some say the early Irish language had its origins in Sanskrit, and that the earliest Celtic serpentine designs had their origins in India, or even Persia.

The early Celts controlled all Europe as far as the Danube, including Budapest, Paris, Belgrade and Lyons. The Roman Legions, with their iron discipline, broke the power of what were to them the "barbaric" Celts, i.e. they did not speak Latin. The Imperial policy of divide and rule put an end to these war-like warriors, with the only exception that Roman civilisation never crossed the sea to Ireland. This was ultimately Ireland's gain, as she missed the Roman military occupation, with its straight Roman military roads, driven through the virgin forests like modern motorways, linking military fort to military fort. Ireland did not enjoy the doubtful benefits of Roman "Law and Order", which crucified all opposition with the mailed fist of a totalitarian state, more often than not headed by power-hungry or insane military generals. They missed Roman sanitation, hot baths, piped water, vomitoriums, mosaic floors and cool villas, and the law and order of the graveyard. The naked Celtic warrior was his own man, an individualist; unity with his neighbours was never his strong point.

The Southern part of Ireland had, geographically, sea routes and links with the Celts of Gaul and Spain, the Bretons and the Basques, and there was constant coming and going in wares between the Celts of Wales and of Ireland, who could look across the Irish Sea at each other's mountain peaks. The nearest Celts were just across the sea in Scotland, a mere ten miles away.

Celtic Ireland was Gaelic speaking, and the many invasions of Ireland by Celtic peoples from Britain and from the Continent took place finally in four phases, between 600 BC and 100 BC. The first were the Picts, followed by the Fir Bolg – who came from Continental Europe – followed by the invaders who founded Leinster and Connacht.

The oldest Gaels, from Scotland, founded Ulster, and the fourth Gaelic division of Ireland was the Province of Munster.

Although the Romans regarded the Celts as barbarians, this Gaelic-speaking race of fighting men had a highly developed civilisation of its own, in addition to its own language. Its society was led by petty kings and princes or chieftains, who in turn were supported by the modern equivalent of law-makers, recorders of history, Druidic priests and magicians and, most important of all, a bardic class, or class of poets. Since the very beginning of the Celtic nation, poets who could break a man by ridicule, or make him by praise, were mighty powerful in the Gaelic society. Magic and poetry went hand in hand, and poets were also all-powerful as soothsayers, or seers, or wielders of supernatural and visionary powers. Kings and princes and petty chieftains needed genealogical support for their power, and for the boosting of their families, and the bards always obliged in filling up the gaps, going as far back as Adam and Eve for ancestry, if necessary. The heritage was in the spoken word, and the written word came much later. History really begins with the written word, the first written words being largely concerned with heroic stories and legends, the exploits of warriors and the loves of kings and queens.

In these earliest days there were no real High Kings of All-Ireland, but there was a multiplicity of small kings, each with his own "tuath" or "tribe", a small realm based on a society of kinship. It was a male-dominated world; a pagan tribal system with a highly developed sense of law and justice, and it produced masterpieces of art from its ranks of craftsmen in metal and leather, and wood and stone.

The worship of the early Celts is obscure and mysterious. They certainly had gods of the sun and of the sea, and held an overwhelming superstition of the nature of the world around them, in rocks and rivers, stones and trees, mountains and clouds, and in the elements. Living on a western Atlantic seaboard, their whole life was bent by the winds and gales, storms and rain clouds, and sun-bursts, in the forever changing movement of clouds and skies from west to east. They were a sensuous people, fully in tune with mother earth.

Perhaps a bloodthirsty lot, they had no tremendous regard as warriors for their own skin, and flung themselves into battle without a qualm or fear of death. This bravado in battle, and almost throw-away attitude to death, as long as it was in a worthwhile encounter, appears to have been a basic attitude of the Celtic warrior. Basically "one far fierce hour and sweet" was preferable to a lifetime of hum-drum mediocrity. Lurking always in the Celtic mind was the concept that it was the man who endured the most who was the victor, not the man who inflicted the most, and the individual conscience concerning this ultimately became accepted by the majority as the philosophy of political endurance, and survival.

Interest in our Celtic heritage was seriously shown by Irish scholars in Victorian times, who were searching for "roots". More often than not, even with great scholarship behind them, they took the romantic view that the Celts were all "... a mighty race, taller than Roman spears", of bearded, heavily armed warriors, with trews or saffron kilts, holding gigantic Irish wolf-hounds on leashes, the sun bursting from the heavens, the older warriors playing chess, listening to the sound of harps, or pipes, or the declaiming of poets, or bards, and stately Irish matrons and maidens in adoring attendance, with great sides of venison, wild boar, salmon, trout, or what-have-you, at the table, while the "Uisce Beatha" – the "water of life" flowed gently, but not too freely, and the forerunners of modern tourists thronged the festive board for free.

Celtic life was not quite as simple as that, of course, but at least when the professional warriors went to war with each other there was no great loss of life, and ordinary life went on with minor "Donnybrooks" in the background. The entire tribe was not involved while a few head of cattle were lost or won, or a wife or two, or a supposed wrong righted. As ever, this Celtic society was a hotbed of lawyers interpreting the "Brehon Laws" with all the arts and skills of modern Senior Counsels or, as they are called in the North of Ireland, Queen's Counsellors. Forever arguing, for the sheer sake and pleasure of discussion, the Great Gaels in their democracy of elected kings and princes, did a great trade in slaves, and were utterly devoted to the tribal ownership of land. The whole history of Ireland is wrapped up with the question of land for the people, and the cynics will say that after centuries of fighting for the possession of their lands, the people did not over-exert themselves in the tilling of their soil. It was enough to have won it, and to hold it, and to guard it jealously against land-hungry neighbours, or foreigners.

However, to talk of "Celts" with a Gaelic language, conscious of a land called "Ireland" is to jump ahead some thousands of years.

The very first people to come to Ireland came between 6,000 and 5,000 BC, after the Ice Age, and were coastal fishermen and gatherers of food. Shells and stone axes mark some of their dwelling places, and while their homes are lost, their tombs remain and are many. From pre-Christian times one can trace up to

40,000 forts, raths or "fairy rings" throughout the length and breadth of modern Ireland. Archaeologically, Ireland is the wealthiest country in Europe, because modern industrialisation and urbanisation have not blotted out the landscape or concreted over man's antiquities. The earliest tombs were megalithic, that is made of "great stones". The most mysterious and mystic of the counties of Ireland is County Sligo, whose landscape abounds in these earliest types of burial chambers.

The Boyne Valley has the most spectacular Passage-Grave tombs in the country, at Newgrange, Dowth and Knowth. Literally, there is a passage into the heart of the mound, and within the stone-roofed mound, a central chamber with burial stones and basins, in many cases highly decorated with Oriental motifs. Bodies were cremated before burial in the tombs.

In addition to these Passage-Graves, there are hundreds of Druidic altars, known as Dolmens. These are enormous standing stones, superimposed on which are huge flat stones roofing the whole. These must surely mark the last resting place of great chiefs or leaders. In addition to these Passage-Graves and Dolmens, there are numerous "Crannogs" or lake dwelling forts. As in many parts of Europe, there are plenty of stone circles and pillar stones. These last-mentioned, tall standing stones, are frequently marked by "Ogham" writing, the earliest form of writing in Ireland. Lines are cut in the stone across a basic line, and the Gaelic names of once famous chiefs and leaders are simply commemorated.

Ireland's Bronze Age, a thousand years before Christ, and as recent as 500 BC, produced some of the most beautiful copper, bronze and gold work in Europe. Hill forts and ring forts sheltered families and their cattle, and one of the most striking of these is the Grianan of Aileach in County Donegal. This is breathtaking in its setting, overlooking Loughs Foyle and Swilly. The walls are 13 feet thick and over 70 feet in diameter. It is an immense ramparted fort and to stand within this stone circle is to sense the presence of the pagan gods of legendary times, and of a people of long ago.

It is only rivalled in its awesomeness by the Fort of Dun Aenghus, on the Aran Islands in County Galway. Set on a cliff edge, with a 200 foot drop into the raging waters of the Atlantic Ocean, this has three half circles of stone wall defences. Beyond these defences of the most westerly fortress in Europe is a field of thousands upon thousands of standing stones, like the earliest form of tank trap in the world. The earliest peoples picked their fortified dwellings in strategic places, often siting them on promontories of land where sea and cliffs and high lands would make for natural defences.

Possibly the most famous single stone in Ireland is the Turoe Stone in County Galway, highly decorated with Celtic curvilinear designs. This is clear evidence of La Tène Celts dwelling in Ireland about one hundred years before Christ. The Turoe Stone is at Bullaun, near Loughrea. This stone originally stood beside the ring-fort of Feerwore.

A Celtic Ireland, with four historic provinces of Ulster, Munster, Leinster and Connacht, (Ulster being predominant in actual power) and divided into about one hundred and fifty small kingships, was fully ready for Christianity, when it came from Rome, via Britain, first in the person of Palladius, a bishop sent by Pope Celestine, followed by Saint Patrick, who became the patron saint of Ireland by virtue of his extraordinarily successful missionary work in converting the pagan kings and princes and populace to Christ. He himself had been captured by raiding pirates, and brought to Ulster as a slave. He escaped back to his native Britain, urged by a calling to convert the native Irish to Christ, and returned as a missionary bishop. To the credit of the Celts they made no martyrs among the missionaries, they very simply went head over heels into the Christian faith with all the fervour of the early Church, and of the desert fathers. They were hermit-like by nature and environment.

The Golden Age of Ireland then followed, when the country was bursting with monastic foundations, universities of great learning, where the faith was kept alive, and ultimately taken back by Irish missionaries to Britain, to Gaul, to Germany, until the whole of Europe was restored from its barbarism to civilisation. This was 6th, 7th and 8th century Ireland, and the monuments, proof, are still to be seen today in the ruins of monastic-university settlements, the round towers, the Celtic crosses and, later, the great art treasures, such as the Book of Kells and Saint Patrick's bell shrine, the Ardagh Chalice and the Cross of Cong.

The round towers, many still standing today, are unique architecturally to Ireland. Approximately 100 feet in height, round and with a pointed conical top, they date from the ninth century, and were bell towers, look-out towers, and places of defence and refuge from the raiding Norsemen. The entrance doors, high above ground level, were reached by rope or ladder, and sacred vessels, books and valuables were stored safely during hit-and-run raids on the coast and the estuaries. There are seventy still standing, many of them on the sites of former university monastic settlements.

The famous Celtic crosses date from the tenth to the thirteenth century, and many are remarkable for their stone-carved, scriptural scenes. They were the visual aids of their day to Christian teaching.

A brief glance at the history of Ireland, after her glorious Golden Age, shows that the Vikings progressed from hit-and-run raids to the permanent settlement of towns such as Dublin, and engaged heavily in trade, including the slave trade. Came the Normans, in the eleventh and twelfth centuries, who, like their Norse relations and predecessors, became absorbed into the nation. The old Gaelic power, headed by the Ulster chiefs, was broken once and for all at the Battle of Kinsale in 1601, and the roots put down for future problems by the confiscation of lands from the people, and the "planting" of loyal English and Scottish Protestant colonists, who remained a beleagured garrison force aloof from the native Irish. From then on, the Irish Parliament was subject to the English Parliament.

From the eighteen hundreds until the nineteen twenties, insurrections, albeit unsuccessful, were the order of the day, alongside a nineteenth century use of the Irish representation in the British Parliament. No nation in Europe has a monopoly of suffering, or starvation, or oppression, but Ireland certainly endured her worst times in the 1840's famine, which decimated her population by starvation, and drove millions to seek a new life in Britain, and notably in the United States of America.

When the democratic process failed to procure Home Rule through Westminster, the young men took to arms, and in 1916, after the rising of the poets, and the citizen army, public opinion swung behind the young Republicans. After a vicious guerilla war between the forces of the Crown and the Irish Republican forces, a Treaty was signed, under duress, and modern Ireland finished up with an "Irish Free State" of twenty-six counties, and a "Northern Ireland" made up of six of the historic nine counties of the Province of Ulster. This latter had its own Parliament for fifty years. Came civil rights agitation from the under-represented section of the people, a dubiously treated minority, and fresh political problems, as yet unresolved, arose. At present Northern Ireland is under the direct rule of Westminster, and is part of the United Kingdom.

Eventually, men of goodwill, of patience, tolerance, mutual respect and understanding, will write another chapter, and a happy one, in the history of an ever youthful, vibrant nation, which plays its part in the heart of the European Community, and in the United Nations.

THE COUNTIES OF IRELAND

Ireland today retains its four ancient provinces of Leinster, Munster, Connacht and Ulster. Politically, twenty-six counties comprise the Republic, and of the nine counties of Ulster, six: Antrim, Down, Armagh, Derry, Tyrone and Fermanagh make up Northern Ireland. Ulster, in the north, is made up of nine counties, Leinster in the east, twelve counties, Connacht, in the west, five counties, and Munster in the south, six counties.

Any journey through Ireland is best done as long

ago by the High Kings. They swept around the countryside clock-wise, commencing in the east, down to the south and south-west, up the west coast, and then around the north. In theory as in history, the greatest power lay for a long time in Ulster, with Leinster a seat of central authority, which did not cover the whole country, and with Munster and Connacht the remotest from central control.

Dublin County is much unexplored by the modern-day traveller, and still contains many pleasant surprises. North of Dublin lies the land of the Fair Strangers, the Norsemen, whose descendants include the hospitable and hard-working market gardeners and fishermen of Rush, and Skerries. Saint Patrick is associated with the island named after him, near Skerries, and Baldongan Castle, three miles distant, is a former power centre of the mysterious and secret society of the Norman Knights Templar. At Lusk is a sixth century round tower, in a state of perfect preservation, to which has been added a square Norman tower. At Swords is another round tower, where once stood the monastery of Saint Colmcille. From the top of the hill of Howth there is a spectacular panoramic view of Dublin Bay, with the Wicklow mountains to the south and the mountains of Mourne to the north. In this area, too, is one of the earliest churches in the country, the Church of Saint Doulagh, near Portmarnock.

South of Dublin is the town of Dun Laoghaire, "The Fort of Leary", the main harbour for Dublin. There is an appropriate monument to George IV at the harbour, to commemorate his visit in 1821 when the town was, on this occasion, given the royal title of "Kingstown". The Martello Tower at Sandycove, now a museum, was the one-time home of James Joyce and his cronies. Killiney Bay is said to be the Naples of Ireland because of its hill and panoramic background of mountains, and its fine sweep of bay.

Adjacent to Dublin County is the Garden of Ireland, County Wicklow, with rolling green country-side, wooded glens and valleys, and low-lying mountains. At Powerscourt are the world-famous gardens, and at Glendalough is the famous monastic settlement of Saint Kevin, dating from the sixth century. The magnificent round tower still stands from the ninth century, guarding the blue lakes – Glendalough means "the Glen of the Two Lakes". The poet-musician-singer, Thomas Moore, made the Vale of Avoca and its village famous in his melody the "Meeting of the Waters".

West Wicklow has the charming village of Blessington, and nearby the huge lake of Pollaphuca, which supplies Dublin city with water and electrical energy.

County Wexford, sweeping round the south-eastern corner of Ireland, is the meeting place of the Irish Sea and the Atlantic Ocean. It is a county of great agricultural tradition, long sandy beaches and broad rivers. The beach at Courtown consists of over two miles of sand, and a few miles away are the sandy beaches of Ballymoney and the delightful coves of Pollshone and of Ardamine. At Ferns, Saint Aidan founded his monastery in the sixth century; later, for a short time, this became the capital of the Kings of Leinster.

Five miles or so from the historic town of Ferns is the village of Boolavogue, which was the scene of a famous insurrection sparked off by the burning of a local chapel. The ballad named after the village has become one of the historic and poignant songs of Ireland, and was loved and much sung and favoured by John F. Kennedy, a former President of the United States. Enniscorthy, in the valley of the River Slaney, is now more famous for its Strawberry Fair than its stormy history. Enniscorthy Castle, dated 1586, was built by the Norman adventurer, Raymond le Gros, then became the property of the MacMurrough Kavanaghs, who gave it to the Franciscans, who were forced to part with it to the Elizabethan poet, Edmund Spencer. At Vinegar Hill, east of the town, the insurrection sparked off in Boolavogue, in 1798, came to its disastrous and cruel end when the untrained peasant army, with its long barrelled duck guns and home-made pikes, fell to professional red-coats and Hessian mercenaries.

Wexford, the capital of the county, is a picturesque town on the mouth of the Slaney, part fishing village, part almost mediaeval, and the home of some of the most talented and kindly people in Ireland. While battles long ago may be remembered in more than a few famous ballads, the town today has world fame as the centre for an international Festival of Opera. A statue of Commodore Barry, founder of the United States Navy, looks out over the harbour. At Dunganstown, not far from New Ross, is the original cottage home of the great-grandfather of John F. Kennedy.

Across the bridge from Wexford Town is Ferrycarrig, the site of an ancient castle where the first Norman invader, Robert Fitzstephen, set up his centre of power with his freebooters. The world can be grateful to Wexford for its wildfowl reserve, where half the Greenland white-fronted geese of the world spend their winter months. Off the coast are the Saltee Islands, one of the largest bird sanctuaries in the country.

Kilkenny, from the Irish for "Canice's Church", a sixth century monastic foundation, still maintains today a liberal and progressive Christian outlook, and is the headquarters of the Design Centre of Ireland. It is a handsome city, with its thirteenth century cathedral, its magnificent castle of the Butlers, the Dukes of Ormonde, and a college which produced Dean Swift, Congreve, Berkeley and Farquhar. In its heyday it was the city of an independent sixteenth century Irish parliament, complete with Papal Nuncio. The cathedral boasts a round tower. Kilkenny is a rich, much under-rated county, whose valleys of the River Nore and of the River Barrow are vales of quiet beauty. The hills of Slieveardagh and of Booley make for attractive uplands.

One of the jewels of the county is Jerpoint Abbey, founded in 1158 by the King of Ossory, Donagh MacGillapatrick. It is the finest monastic ruins in the country.

Adjacent to the county of Kilkenny is the county of Carlow, to the north-east. Barely 300 miles square it is nearly the smallest county in Ireland, which, of course, is "the wee county", County Louth. With the help of the River Slaney, and of the River Barrow, it has a rich fertile limestone land, and the landscape has soft-shaped hills and a great greenness.

The county capital is Norman, and the countryside has memorials four thousand years old, such as the Dolmen at Browne's Hill, two miles from Carlow, with the largest capstone in Europe, twenty feet square, five feet thick and weighing one hundred tons.

Inland counties of Ireland are all too often neglected, or overlooked, by people speeding through them to somewhere else, and County Kildare is one such county. West of Dublin, it has been the horse land of sporting, racing and hunting people since before the time of Christ. The rolling grasslands, over limestone plains, produce the greatest race horses in the world.

The national stud is there, and the finest Georgian mansion in the country, Castletown House, now the headquarters of the Georgian Society of Ireland. The Curragh is the leading race track, and on this course each year is held the Irish Derby, which carries one of the largest prize monies of any classic in Europe.

Three places spring to mind at the mention of Kildare: Celbridge, once the home of Esther Vanhomrigh, Jonathan Swift's tragic Vanessa; Maynooth, with its college of Saint Patrick, one of the largest and most conservative Catholic seminaries in the world, and Conolly's Folly, near Celbridge, one of the most obscene wastes of money and labour by a worthless and useless landlord class.

The county of Laois, flat, save for the Slieve Bloom mountains, has as its main town Port Laois – "the fort of Laoghis" – and was originally called Maryborough after its settlement by Bloody Mary in her attempt to subdue the clan of the O'Mores.

Offaly, the adjacent county, in addition to its fame for "Tullamore Dew", the Irish equivalent of Drambuie, has, on the banks of the Shannon, one of the most famous holy places in Ireland, Clonmacnois, the monastery and university city founded by Saint Ciaran in the year 548 AD. The stone Cross of the Scriptures is one of the most ornate of all Celtic crosses, and the whole area is a riot of stone crosses, early grave slabs and sites of ancient churches and cathedrals.

The county of Westmeath, with its many wooded lakes and rivers, is famous for its "Goldsmith Country" near Lough Ree, described in his "The Deserted Village"; and for the town of Athlone, where John Count McCormack, one of the world's greatest tenors, was born.

Longford, a small county of lakes, rivers and farms, is for ever associated with Edgeworthstown; the famous family whose members included Maria Edgeworth, first settled there, and their family vault is in the attractive and well-kept Church of Saint John. Goldsmith, too, is associated with this county, which gave him the idea for his play "She Stoops to Conquer".

The county of Meath, "Royal" Meath, was the seat of pagan and Christian kings at historic Tara, and it was on the Hill of Slane that Saint Patrick lit the Paschal Fire. Trim, Navan and Kells are the best-known historic towns, and Kells was the monastic settlement of Saint Colmcille of the sixth century.

The round tower at Kells is 100 feet high, and the most valuable book in the world, the Book of Kells, was produced in this monastic settlement. The Celtic crosses in the area are exceedingly ornate.

County Louth, the smallest county in the country, just over 300 square miles, has the distinction of being associated with one of the great epics of ancient Ireland, the Táin Bó Cuailgne – "The Cattle Raid of Cooley". It is rich in historic monuments and noted for its Cistercian Abbey ruins of Mellifont, founded by Saint Malachi, the Irish friend of the great Saint Bernard of Clairvaux. It is equally famous for the fifth century monastery of Monasterboice – "Saint Buithe's Abbey" – where Muireadach's cross is one of the most exquisite stone carvings of the earliest Christian period.

South-west of the Province of Leinster are the six counties of the Province of Munster, beginning with Waterford, adjacent to Wexford and Kilkenny. A county of rivers, the Suir and the Blackwater, its prides are the Comeragh mountains and a rugged coastline. The city of Waterford is a Norse-Norman foundation and it has given many distinguished leaders of thought and of action to the nation. Ardmore, on the sea, was the seventh century monastery of Saint Declan, and is marked by a perfectly preserved round tower. Lismore Castle, on the River Blackwater, is one of the most attractive-looking in Ireland, and dates back over the centuries to an early Christian monastery, taken over by King John, and then by the rapacious Sir Walter Raleigh and the Earl of Cork "Boyle's Law" family.

County Cork, the largest county in Ireland, has probably produced more brains, beauty and talent per square acre than any other county in Ireland. With an enormous indented Atlantic coastline, and with one of the most spectacular waterways, the Blackwater, its capital city was founded by Saint Finbarr as a monastic university in the sixth century, and near this original site the present-day University College, Cork, stands. A "Rebel" city, Cork has always given the lead to the nation. Five miles from the city is the village and castle of Blarney, with its famous stone, said to give the gift of eloquence to all who kiss it. To the east of Cork is the village of Youghal, famous for the house in which Sir Walter Raleigh lived, and which still stands today. Kinsale, to the South, once one of the most important British naval ports, is associated with William Penn, founder of the State of Pennsylvania and one time Clerk of the Admiralty Court of Kinsale.

West Cork revels in wild and rugged scenery and becomes an area of warm beauty and soft Mediterranean-type flora and fauna in places such as Bantry Bay, Glengarriff, Gougane Barra and the Beara Peninsula.

The county next door, Kerry, is a blend of mountains and cliffs and spectacular Atlantic headlands. Always the most remote south-westerly county in Ireland, it has kept to a high degree the ancient tradition of the country for hospitality, for learning and for strength of character. The Iveragh and Dingle Peninsulas are the next promontories to America, and the beauty of the lakes of Killarney has never ceased to capture the admiration of the world. It is very probable that Saint Brendan, known as The Navigator, set forth from Dingle and discovered the coast of America long before Columbus.

County Limerick, north of Kerry and Cork, and on the historic River Shannon, is so rich a county that it is known as "The Golden Vale". Originally a Danish settlement, the city of Limerick is a well preserved Irish town. In the country, twelve miles to the south of the City, is Lough Gur, one of the most ancient dwelling places in the land. All the ages are recorded in the many stone monuments and remains of dwelling places, from Neolithic to Norman times. Across the broad estuary of the Shannon is the mighty limestone area of the Burren and the land of the 700 foot high Cliffs of Moher, and the fascinating strand of Lahinch, County Clare. This is O'Brien country, and the one-time haunt of the MacNamara Clan. The Burren landscape is like a moon-scape, with an extraordinary range of flora, much of it Mediterranean and alpine.

There remains one more county to add to the list of Munster counties – one made famous by a World War I marching song – "It's a long way to Tipperary". The mountain ranges of the Galtees and the Knockmealdowns are of great beauty, over 2,000 feet in height. The lush grasslands of the Golden Vale, through which flows the River Suir, yield great agricultural wealth. Clonmel is for ever associated with the famous patriot Father Nicholas Sheehy, but the glories of Tipperary include the Mitchelstown

Caves, the castle of Cahir, the Glen of Aherlow, and its crowning glory – the Irish Acropolis – The Rock of Cashel. Cashel takes its name from the Irish for "The Stone Fort of Munster". This limestone rock rises over 200 feet above the plain and was the power centre of the Kings of Munster from the third until the eleventh century. Saint Patrick's Cross, Cormac's Chapel and towers show Irish church architecture at its peak.

"Walk Tall" might well be the motto of the men of Tipperary; mountain men, who have contributed more than their share to the building of the nation. Slievenamon – "The Mountain of the Women of Feimhinn" – is associated with the ancient legend of Diarmuid and Grainne, while at Holy Cross stands the well-preserved and restored eleventh century Abbey.

Roscommon is one of Connacht's most lake-strewn counties. Entirely inland, it is bounded on its eastern side by the River Shannon and its lakes. Lough Key, with its forest park, is typical of the area. Lough Gara is rich in archaeological finds, ancient dug-outs, crannogs, and a magnificent dolmen.

The hill of Rathcroghan is reputed to have been the power centre of Queen Maeve of Connacht, who features in the Ulster war saga of the "Táin Bó Cuailgne" – "The Cattle Raid of Cooley". Probably a royal capital in its ancient days, it has nearby the Burial Place of the Kings, where Conn of a Hundred Battles and three famous queens, Banba, Fodhla and Eire lie. Dathi, an early Irish pagan king has his monument too.

Elphin was the birthplace of Oliver Goldsmith and Castlerea the birthplace of Sir William Wilde, father of Oscar Wilde.

At Clonalis is a Victorian-looking mansion, Clonalis House, home of the O'Conor Don, a direct descendant of the last king of Ireland around 1169. The house is a treasure trove of historical documents, paintings, books and furnishings.

Leitrim is a lake-land county, and, because it is a relatively small county, on the borders of Sligo and Roscommon, is not as well known as its beauty deserves it to be. Lough Allen divides the county neatly in two parts ·Dromahair – "The Ridge of the Two Air-Demons" – is the turbulent country of the Clan O'Rourke and recalls the intensely dramatic story of Dervorgilla, wife of Tiernan O'Rourke, who went off with Dermot MacMurrough, King of Leinster. This incident was the reason why the Anglo-Normans and their Welsh free-booters were invited from South Wales to "assist" Dermot against his neighbouring chiefs, and so set in motion the Norman invasion of Ireland.

Little known, but of great beauty, are the Glencar waterfall and Lough, and the mountains of Truskmore and Cloghcorragh, and Lough Allen, seven miles long and three miles wide.

The county of Sligo, Yeats' country, has, on Lough Gill, near the town of Sligo, the lake-island of Innis-free, and a host of places associated with the poet. Lough Arrow is of equal beauty, and the whole area is steeped in great antiquities, since from earliest times it was the coastal route for armies marching north and south.

Lough Gill has its megalithic tomb, and on top of Knocknarea is the tomb of Queen Maeve of Connacht. Over six hundred feet in circumference, and eighty feet high, it can be seen for miles around.

Drumcliff was the site of a monastery founded by Saint Columba in AD 574, and there is a magnificent early Celtic cross, and the grave of W. B. Yeats. The mountain of Benbulben dominates the county, and on its slopes died Diarmuid, the hero of the Diarmuid and Grainne love epic. Drumcliff was the scene of a famous early Christian battle which established the law of copyright. Three thousand men died fighting for Saint Columba versus Saint Finian in the "Battle of the Books". Finian had given Columba a loan of a psalter, and Columba made a copy from it, which Finian claimed as his property. The matter was referred to the High King who, Solomon-wise, judged: "To every cow its calf and to every book its copy". The plain of Moytura was the scene of many, many battles in the centuries before Christ.

Galway county, lying on the Western Atlantic sea-board, is the chocolate-box colour photograph idea of everybody's Ireland, with its Twelve Bens of Connemara and its famous Lough Corrib. It is probable that Ptolemy referred to Galway city as "Magnata". In Norman times the city became "The City of the Tribes" – fourteen of them, and for many years the city traded with Spain, so that its buildings and people have a distinctive Spanish look. Off the coast are the Aran Islands, made famous in drama by J. M. Synge's "Rides to the Sea", and in film in Flaherty's documentary "Man of Aran". Lough Corrib, seven miles wide and twenty-seven in length, dominates much of the country's scenery. At Clifden, on the edge of the sea, the first east-west trans-Atlantic flight landed in 1919. Clonfert is a monastic settlement founded by Saint Brendan the Navigator in the fifth century.

Not far from the town of Loughrea is the Turoe Stone, a perfect example of La Tene art of one hundred years before Christ. Coole Park is forever associated with Lady Gregory of the Abbey Theatre fame, Thoor Ballylee with W. B. Yeats, and Ballinahinch with "Humanity Dick", the founder of the R.S.P.C.A.

The county of Mayo has a fantastic Atlantic coast-line, a huge and magnificent off-shore island – Achill – and a lofty mountain – Croagh Patrick – Saint Patrick's Mountain, over 2,500 feet high. Clare Island was the fortress home of the Irish Pirate cum Sea Queen of the West – Grace O'Malley. At Westport is one of the finest stately homes in Ireland open to the public. Ballintubber Abbey has a history of uninterrupted service from the twelfth century until the present day.

South Moytura, plain of a thousand pre-Christian battles, merges with North Moytura in Sligo.

Of the nine counties of Ulster, Donegal, the most north-easterly, separated from its hinterland of Derry by the political borderline of Northern Ireland, is the jewel. It abounds in sweeping sandy beaches, washed by the Atlantic Ocean, and Donegal town was the seat of the O'Donnell Clan, of whom the most famous was Red Hugh. Lough Derg – the Red Lake – is the legendary penitential place of Saint Patrick. Lough Finn is the scene of ancient warrior sagas, and the Grianan of Aileach is an awesome circular stone fort, built nearly two thousand years before the birth of Christ. Saint Colmcille was born on the shores of Gartan Lough in AD 521. Mount Errigal, almost two and a half thousand feet high, and cone-shaped in gleaming white, looks for all the world like a volcanic mountain in Japan. For sheer beauty of mountain, lake, valley and peninsular coastline, Donegal is probably the most glamorous county in Ireland.

The county of Derry is part of the historic province of Ulster, and politically, today, part of the six counties of Northern Ireland. The capital city, Derry, or Londonderry as it became called when James I granted it to the Irish Society of London, was originally called Derry-Calgach, that is "Calgach's Oak Wood". Saint Colmcille, perhaps better known throughout Europe as Saint Columbanus, set up a monastic foundation and university in AD 546, and cleared the original oak wood for his settlement. James I re-built the original city, and made it a walled city, which has survived the many vicissitudes of history. One of the most famous of Irish traditional pieces of music is the "Londonderry" or "Derry" Air, which was first written down in Limavady, in the County of Derry, in 1851, from an itinerant fiddler.

It is a county of hills and lowlands in the north, and glens and valleys, with the Sperrin Mountains in the south. At Coleraine is the newest of Ireland's universities. The Northern Atlantic beaches are beautiful, and the county shares its borders with Donegal in the north-east, with Antrim in the east, and with Tyrone in the south. Coleraine is associated with Saint Patrick, and Maghera has its sixth century church of Saint Lurach.

Bordering Derry is the magnificent coastal county of Antrim, just thirteen miles from Torr Head across to the coast of Scotland. Lough Neagh, the largest lake in Ireland, or in Great Britain, takes up the west of the county, and the rest is fertile valleys and hills, and rising land. Belfast city, the capital of Northern Ireland, is an enormous industrial area and port. The Antrim coastal road is one of the most attractive in the whole of Ireland, and the county retains its world fame for two things, the Irish whiskey distilled at Bushmills, and the extraordinary rock formation of cooled lava which constitutes the Giant's Causeway. It was on the mountain of Slemish that the slave boy, later to become Saint Patrick, spent six or so years tending sheep.

County Armagh, south of Antrim and Lough Neagh. is justly famous as "The Garden of Ulster". The town of Armagh – "Ard Macha" – Macha's Height, is named after the battling Queen Macha who, three hundred years before Christ, ruled from her royal palace at Eamhain Macha. Saint Patrick naturally chose this ancient town as his primatial see, and founded the monastic university of Armagh. Slieve Gullion, in South Armagh, nearly two thousand feet in height, is the site of Bronze Age burial places. Portadown is the breeding ground of some of the world's finest roses, and famous for its splendid apple crops.

County Monaghan shares the distinction with Counties Donegal and Cavan, of being south of the "Border", and is a charming hilly lake-land, with well tended farms. This is the county of the Clan MacMahon, and the birthplace of the famous poet, Patrick Kavanagh. Near the town of Monaghan is Tydavnet, associated with Saint Dympna, daughter of a pagan king who ruled in this area which was historically part of the old kingdom of Oriel. In the west of the county is the town of Clones, one time a monastic settlement founded by Saint Tighearnach in the fifth century. The village of Inishkeen was the site of a monastery founded by Saint Deagh in the sixth century.

County Down is famous in ballad and song for its "Star of the County Down", and its "Mountains of Mourne". It is a rich county, probably the most fertile land in the whole of Ireland, contrasted by the granite mountains of the Mourne. Eastwards, the peninsula of Ards forms a natural barrier between the sea and Strangford Lough. The coastal resorts of Bangor, Donaghadee, Newcastle and Warrenpoint line the eastern magnificent sea boundary of the county.

Holywood, six or so miles from Belfast, was originally the site of a church founded by the seventh century Saint Laserian. The Normans named it "Sanctus Boscus" – the "Holy Wood".

Bangor – the "Peaked Hill" – was originally a monastic foundation in the fifth century, of Saint Comgall. A major university city, its most illustrious graduate was Saint Columbanus, who founded monasteries throughout Europe, and another was Saint Gall, who brought Christianity to the Swiss. Some idea of the enormous size of this university settlement may be seen from the fact that when the Norsemen destroyed it in the eighth century, they put to the sword some three thousand people.

Donaghadee takes its name from the Irish for "The Church of Saint Diach".

The Ards Peninsula is of great beauty, and Newtownards, a town of mediaeval origin, has on its eastern boundary the site of a monastery founded by

Saint Finian, in the sixth century.

The star of the county is, of course, Downpatrick – "Dun Phadraig" – Saint Patrick's Fort. He founded his earliest church here. The saint landed at Saul, two miles north-east of Downpatrick in AD 432. It is said that Patrick died at Downpatrick; and the supposed site of his grave is marked by an enormous modern boulder of granite, into which has been cut the name "Patric" and a cross.

Slieve Donard, nearly three thousand feet in height, is the highest of the Mountains of Mourne, and from its summit there is a view to the Isle of Man, to Scotland, to Donegal and to Wicklow.

County Tyrone is bounded on the north-east and north by counties Donegal and Derry, on the east by counties Antrim and Armagh, and in the south-west by the Counties of Fermanagh and Monaghan. This is O'Neill country, with every type of scenery, ranging from the 2,000 foot high Sperrin Mountains, to hills, river valleys and glens.

The O'Neills ruled from Dungannon – "Gannon's Fort". In the Clogher Valley lies the village of Clogher, which was the site of the Cathedral of Saint Macartan, a disciple of Saint Patrick. Near Cookstown is Killymoon Castle, a mansion designed by Nash, and a few miles away, south of Cookstown, is the territory of the O'Hagan Clan. To the east lies Ardboe, where Saint Colman of Dromore founded a monastery in the sixth century. It has one of the most outstanding Celtic crosses in Ulster.

The town of Omagh is set on the rivers Drumragh and Camowen, which join together to form the River Strule.

The town of Strabane – "The Fair River-Meadow", on the River Mourne, has many distinguished sons, not the least of whom was John Dunlap, who printed the American Declaration of Independence. The printing house of Gray's, where he learnt his printing trade, is still in existence.

County Cavan, part of the twenty-six counties of the Irish Republic, is the home of the O'Reilly Clan. It is lake-land countryside, with the River Erne rising in Lough Gowan on its way North. Near the pretty town of Virginia, which is on the side of Lough Ramor, is Cuilcagh Lough, and in the house that once stood nearby, Cuilcagh House, Dean Swift sat down to begin his writing of "Gulliver's Travels". Cavan has produced many famous journalists, and at least two great generals, Field Marshal Thomas Brady of the Austrian Army, who became Governor of Dalmatia, born at Cootehill, and General Phil Sheridan, born at Killinkere, a commander-in-chief of the Army of the United States of America. On the west side of Cuilcagh Mountain is the "Shannon Pot", the source of the mighty River Shannon.

What makes the county of Fermanagh so superbly different is that the River Erne covers a vast area with its Upper and Lower Loughs. Enniskillen, the home of the Maguire Clan, stands loftily in between the two beautiful lakes. It shares the Cuilcagh Mountain with its Cavan border, and north-west shares Lough Melvin. On the western border are the Upper and Lower Lough Macnean.

A few miles North of Enniskillen is Devenish Island on the Lower Lough Erne. Here is another Clonmacnoise, with the sixth century monastery founded by Saint Molaise. There is a splendid round tower, eighty-five feet high, extensive monastic and mediaeval ruins, and a high cross. On White Island, north of Devenish, is an early church and sculptures. East of Enniskillen is Killadeas Church with seventh century carvings.

Belleek, on the Donegal border, is world-famous for its chinaware. West Fermanagh has limestone hills, and they contain some of the most complex cave systems in Ireland.

Some nine miles south-west of Enniskillen is Florence Court, the beautiful demesne of the Earl of Enniskillen.

With the County of Fermanagh the clock-wise circuit of the thirty-two counties of Ireland comes to an end.

Errigal right, in County Donegal, is an almost 2,500 feet high mountain composed of quartzite.

In County Donegal, turf cutters above and top left practice their time-honoured way of producing fuel.

A pub interior is shown centre left at Maghery, Donegal, and below two visitors stop to admire the tranquil scenery at nearby Dungloe.

A farmer and his calf bottom left make their way along the beautiful beach at Rossnowlagh, on Donegal Bay, and a young girl takes part in a parade at Killybegs.

Right: tagging sheep prior to turning them out to pasture.

Burton above and above right *is an important fishing village where more salmon and lobster are landed than at any other port in Ireland or Britain. It is also a popular centre for boating trips.*

Fanad Head *left, at the tip of the Fanad Peninsula, has some of the most dramatic cliff scenery in Ireland, including remarkable examples of marine erosion. Between the tortuous inlets of Sheep Haven and Mulroy Bay lies Rosguill Peninsula and Melmore Head below. Glen Head, viewed from Rossan Point centre right, is another of County Donegal's rugged landmarks.*

Sandy beaches and the sheltered waters of Dawross Bay provide a welcome retreat near Rosbeg below right.

The Lake of Glencar left and above consists of
two miles of cascades and waterfalls, the tallest of
which is some fifty feet high. The lake, its environ
above left and the countryside around Sligo
right were much loved by the Sligo Poet, W.B.
Yeats, in whose memory the plaque below has
been erected.

Ashford Castle above right, *owned by an Irish-American millionaire, was formerly the country seat of the Guinness Family (famed for their well-known brew).*

The Burrishoole River above *drains Lough Feeagh and Lough Furnace and provides some of the finest salmon fishing to be found in Ireland, whilst just off the coast of Achill Island* below *a trawler sets out for fishing of a different kind.*

South of Westport, the Partry Mountains, *several thousand feet high, dominate the landscape* right *and an idyllically situated cottage* left *nestles among the ever-varying scenery of County Mayo.*

A solitary boat in Clew Bay *right reflects all the remote charm of a land where donkeys and carts still roam the almost deserted lanes below.*

Even Mayo's largest town, Ballina left, *has remained relatively unspoiled by the fact that it is an excellent angling resort.*

*et in North Mayo, between Foxford, Pontoon and
allina, Lough Conn* above *affords excellent
almon and trout fishing.*

chill, left and centre right, *remote and almost
ntirely covered with heather, is the largest island
f the Irish coast. It is joined to the mainland only
y a bridge.*

he Sheefry Hills above and below right *preside
ramatically over south-west Mayo and Delphi.
ot far from Delphi lies the tranquil Doo Lough
 black lake* below.

ownpatrick Head far left *reaches out into a
elentless sea.*

Lough Key Forest Park *right is a nature trail open to the public. Set deep in the Lakeland of Ireland, it is equipped with a restaurant and caravan park.*

Known as the "Abbey which refused to die", Ballintubber *above has been restored and has remained in use for over 750 years, It was founded by the King of Connaught in the 12th century.*

Westport House *left and below, designed by the famous Georgian architect Richard Castle, was the first Irish stately home to open its doors to the public. The home of the Marquess of Sligo, it contains a magnificent collection of books, paintings, silver and glass.*

Clonalis House *below and left, the home of the most distinguished of Irish families, the O'Connor Don, contains an impressive range of antique books, manuscripts and regalia.*

Headford House above left and right, *the magnificent estate of the Marquess of Headford, lies in wooded land a few miles outside the town of the same name.*

Tullynally Castle left, *near Castlepollard, is the residence of Lord Longford. A spacious castellated mansion, it is mentioned several times under its former name of Pakenham Hall in the memoirs of the 18th century novelist, Maria Edgeworth, whose father was a frequent guest here.*

A rowing boat lies half-concealed among the reeds of Lough Owel *below.*

The River Blackwater above *meanders through lush parkland and wooded valleys in the Royal County, royal because Meath is the county of the Royal Acropolis, the Hill of Tara of the ancient kings.*

Ireland's lush pastures are rich and extensive, its waters abound in fish, but despite the hard manual labour required to make the best of these natural resources, this is a gentle, leisurely land where there is still time for everything... time for a drink or time simply to sit and ruminate.

Turf *centre right* is cheap, readily available and there is enough of it to fuel the local cottage hearths.

Kylemore Abbey *overleaf*, in the charge of hospitable Irish Benedictine Dames, has a reputation for the best teas in Connemara.

Once a 5th century monastic university beside the great waterway of the Shannon River, "Cluain mic nois" left, the "Field of the Son of Nos" is a burial place of kings and saints. It abounds in Celtic architecture, ancient crosses and round towers, among them the magnificent Cross of the Scripture below. The Nun's Church in Clonmacnois above left is a classic example of Hiberno-Romanesque. It was built in 1167 by the repentant and grief-stricken wife of Tiernan O'Rourke.

The beautifully preserved Cloghan Castle right and far right stands north-west of the village of the same name.

Birr Castle above withstood many a siege in the wars of the 16th and 17th centuries. It later became the residence of the earls of Rosse.

Dublin Castle *below, built between 1208 and 1220, was once the residence of the English viceroys.*

Founded in 1190, St. Patrick's Cathedral *left is mainly Early English in style. The original structure was extensively rebuilt towards the end of the 14th century after a fire. In 1320 the Pope founded a university which had its home in the cathedral until it was suppressed by Henry VIII.*

Adjoining St. Patrick's Cathedral, Marsh's Library *above and right, founded by Archibishop Marsh in 1707, is the oldest library in Ireland and contains over 25,000 volumes.*

A fair city indeed, Dublin these pages fittingly boasts some of the nation's most elegant architecture. Lining the banks of the Liffey are such notable buildings as the Four Courts *right* and the old Custom House *below*. Trinity College, Dublin *left*, is Ireland's premier seat of learning, while O'Connell Street *above* is a hive of commercial activity.

Delicate wrought iron, and rust coloured
creepers decorate the elegant Georgian
frontages of Merrion Square's old houses
right. The silhouette of the Custom House
dome above overshadows the Halfpenny
Bridge and the languid waters of the River
Liffey. Seat of Ireland's government is the
reassuringly solid looking Leinster House top
left. The old Parliament House is now home
to the Bank of Ireland and stands on College
Green, facing the entrance to Trinity College
left. The waters of the Grand Canal at
Portobello Lock below provide ideal
facilities for canoeists.

The development and planting of Dublin's famous Phoenix Park *above and below left was* begun in 1740. Today it includes about 1,760 acres of beautifully laid out gardens and trees.

The gateway to Dalkey Island, Coliemore Harbour *right*, is a favourite picnic spot for Dubliners in the summer months.

The Four Courts *below*, on the northern quays of the River Liffey in Dublin, is a magnificent building, begun in 1786 to the design of Thomas Cooley and completed by James Gandon.

Fishing and pleasure boats wait in some of Ireland's more secluded waters *above*.

In its idyllic setting above left, Powerscourt House itself below left, is an imposing 18th century building of hewn granite with a magnificent view of its sloping gardens adorned with statuary, tessellated pavements and ornamental lakes.

Another of County Wicklow's tranquil parklands is the lovely Vale of Clara above on the banks of the meandering Avonmore River.

The countryside near Hollywood right was much loved by Saint Kevin, the Saint of Wicklow.

A round tower still stands at Glendalough, County Wicklow below, the place to which St. Kevin came in the sixth century in search of solitude, and where he lived for many years as a hermit.

Glendalough centre left, *the Valley of the Lakes is where Saint Kevin founded a monastic settlement, remains of which can still be seen.*

Greystones above left *is a seaside resort lying in* [a] *pleasantly wooded part of the Wicklow coast, sou[th] of Bray, and Blainroe Golf Course* above *provid[es] not only excellent sport but also a breathtaking view of Brittas Bay.*

Mount Usher Gardens below, *with their sumptuous collection of sub-tropical plants, are th[e] demesne of the celebrated Walpole family.*

South of Wicklow, the Silver Strand left *is a popular sandy beach surrounded by cliffs.*

Glenmacnass in County Wicklow right *is a beautiful valley walled in by towering mountains through which the Glenmacnass River rushes to join the Avonmore.*

A horse-drawn caravan pauses for a moment on [a] *bridge in Claragh, Wicklow* below.

An imposing statue overlooks the great pass between Limerick and Tipperary overleaf.

Exquisitely restored by the Irish Tourist Board, Cahir Castle *top left and below is basically 15th century. The Earl of Essex, admirer of Good Queen Bess, once captured it more by luck than judgement but since then it has stood in relative peace.*

The Abbey of Holy Cross *centre left dates from the 11th century. It was founded by the King of Thomond and it was here that pilgrims came to venerate a relic of the true cross.*

Once the seat of Munster kings, the Rock of Cashel *below left is a remarkable outcrop of limestone rising 200 feet above the plain and crowned with a magnificent group of ruins. About half a mile west of the rock is the Cistercian Hore Abbey right and above, a daughter house of Mellifont in County Louth.*

Bunratty Castle was once the residence of the O'Briens of Thomond. It was restored in 1960 and furnished with fifteenth and sixteenth century furnishings and now provides the ideal venue for mediaeval banquets *left and below*. The Bunratty Folk Park includes the forge *bottom*. Not far from Ennis, County Clare, Craggaunowen Castle has an impressive museum and a reconstruction of a Bronze Age "crannog" or lake dwelling *above*.

The Cliffs of Moher, County Clare *right* drop 700 feet to the waves thundering below.

dare Manor, Limerick above, above right and *erleaf, a nineteenth century limestone building neo-Gothic style, is the beautifully furnished idence of the Earl of Dunraven.*

he historic village of Adare is also noted for its e monastic ruins left, below and right, *which ll stand not far from the River Maigue.*

On the River Nore in County Kilkenny stands Kilkenny Castle above left, built in the 13th century by the Norman gangster Strongbow. It was subsequently the home of the Butlers, the Dukes of Ormonde.

Jerpoint Abbey left was founded by the King of Ossory in 1158 for the Cistercian order. The church is cruciform, with the usual Cistercian arrangement of two chapels in each transept.

The stained-glass window below is part of St. Canice's Cathedral in Kilkenny, named after the saint who founded the city in the 6th century.

Carlow right, once a stronghold of the Anglo-Normans, is the county town, pleasantly situated on the River Barrow above.

Dunbrody Abbey right *was founded in the 11th century by English monks. In the course of time it became a famous place of sanctuary for anyone on the run from the Kingly authorities.*

Hook Head, County Wexford above right *is a long, narrow, rock-bound peninsula noted for the beauty of the corals found in the carboniferous limestone.*

The walls of the Franciscan Friary left *exude the very history of Ireland's turbulent past. Then, the Wexford friars were known to die to a man rather than relinquish their friary.*

Three miles south of Wexford is Johnstown Castle above, *built in the 13th century by the Anglo-Norman Esmonde family.*

Wexford itself overleaf, *is picturesquely situated where the River Slaney enters Wexford harbour.*

Near Carnsore Point, Lady's Island below *is joined to the mainland by a causeway. Once the site of a monastery dedicated to the Blessed Virgin, it has been a place of pilgrimage for centuries.*

Ardmore, County Waterford *above right was formely a centre of 7th century learning under the leadership of St. Declan.*

Ardmore Round Tower *right is one of the best preserved towers in Ireland and stands almost 100 feet high.*

Erected in 1003 as part of the Danish defence, Reginald's Tower *above still stands at the western end of the quay at Waterford. During the many sieges of Waterford the tower was an inevitable target and its walls still bear the scars of cannon.*

Dunmore *below, the old mail packet station for boats to England, is now a pleasant resort.*

Annestown, County Waterford *right was once the stately defended home and castle of the Power family. Nine miles south-east of Waterford city is* Dunmore East *left, a popular summer retreat at the mouth of Waterford Harbour.*

By night below the Bishop's Palace in Waterford is bathed in floodlight.

The towering form of St. Colman's Cathedral dominates the town of Cobh overleaf, the most important Irish port of call for transatlantic liners.

The strikingly attractive little resort of Glandore has a beautiful outlook over the waters of Glandore Harbour above.

The fishing village of Baltimore, County Cork above right has witnessed a stormy history. This was the setting for Thomas Davis' "Sack of Baltimore", a vivid poetic description of a raid by Algerian Pirates in 1631.

Kinsale is one of the best-equipped sea angling centres on the south coast and its beaches at Summer Cove centre right are ideal for bathing.

Ballycotton below right looks out over the wide inlet of Ballycotton Bay whilst Barley Cove, West Cork below provides an idyllic site for a popular holiday complex. Baltard Bay left is punctuated by the rugged rocks which are so characteristic of this expanse of coastline.

"The Spaniard" above is one of Kinsale's popular pubs and a welcome retreat for the visitors who are drawn to this sea angling centre on the south coast.

Bantry House, formerly the home of the Earls of Bantry left and above and below right is a fine Georgian House built about 1750. It is now open to the public and famous for its art treasures, furnishings and French tapestries.

Blarney Castle and the magic Blarney Stone below, with its traditional power of conferring eloquence on those who kiss it, are world famous. The Blarney Stone is set high up in one of the castle walls and to kiss it one has to lean over backwards from the parapet walk of the battlements.

The St. Patrick's Day Parade in County Cork overleaf is the occasion of a colourful display of talents.

Seen above left *from Sherkin View, Bantry is delightfully situated beneath sheltering hills at the head of famous Bantry Bay.*

The gardens of Garinish Island left *lie off the harbour of Glengarriff. It was here that George Bernard Shaw wrote part of his play "St. Joan".*

Barley Cove above *encloses one of County Cork's most magnificent sandy beaches whilst the spectacular Healy Pass road winds its way across the mountains* right.

Cows graze in the verdant pastures near Mitchelstown, Cork below, *the home of Galtee cheese and butter.*

Road bowling below *is a game peculiar to Cork. Fortunately the organisers warn all traffic and tourists of their intent to "loft" the ball as it is made of iron and would decapitate a fleeing bull at short range.*

Dividing the counties of Kerry and Cork. Gougane Barra right *is the source of the River Lee.*

Schull left *is a small village with a quaint little harbour.*

Killarney, County Kerry *above left is a fairy-tale land of mountains and lakes which has understandably been immortalized by innumerable poets and painters.*

Angling and boating in the lakes and rivers of County Kerry *centre and below left have drawn many visitors to its quiet, pastoral scenery. In particular the 'Ring of Kerry' road provides spectacular views of the mountains* above *as it encircles the Iveragh Peninsula.*

Only the sound of rushing water disturbs the peace of Cummeenduff or "Black Valley" right.

Ross Castle *below, a well-preserved 14th century ruin, is one of the best examples of castle-building in County Kerry. Still formidable in its magnitude, it overlooks the Lower Lake, largest of the Killarney Lakes.*

Coumeenoole Strand *overleaf provides an ideal spot for sunbathing.*

The Muckross Estate in Killarney contains a folk museum, where the blacksmith above demonstrates his skill. Muckross Abbey left was a Franciscan Friary of the 14th century founded by the Mac Carthy, Chief of Desmond. It has been the inspiration of writers such as Sir Walter Scott, Thackeray and Tennyson.

In Kenmare right salmon are smoked to the satisfaction of even the most *discri*minating palate.

Apart from the advent of the motor car, Slea Head left on the Dingle Peninsula has changed little in the last hundred years. Harvesting above and below right, milk delivery centre right and turf collecting below are still carried out by the old traditional methods.

Cahirciveen left is renowned for the enormous church which stands in its main street . . . the Daniel O'Connell memorial church, erected in memory of the great Irish liberator.

Viewed from Coomakista Pass, Derrynane Bay above well illustrates the beauty of Ireland's coastline. Just off the coast, Valentia Island above right is joined to the mainland by an excellent bridge road.

Aghadoe Church, overlooking the Lower Lake right, was built in the 12th century but it incorporates some portions of a church several centuries older.

A jaunting car below is an ideal and leisurely way of travelling on the country lanes of Kerry or even on the "Ring of Kerry" seen below right winding along the rugged coastline.

Belfast City Hall, pictured by night above left, was designed in Renaissance style by Bramwell Thomas and completed in Portland stone in 1906. It contains the Council Chambers and four beautifully designed halls.

The Parliament Building at Stormont below left was erected between 1928 and 1932 by the British Government to house the parliament and certain government ministries of Northern Ireland.

Ballycopeland Windmill below which dates from 1784 still stands, beautifully restored near 'Oilean an Mhuilinn', the Island of the Mill. Kilkeel Harbour, County Down above, is a quiet seaside resort and the headquarters of a large fishing fleet, and Bangor right is one of the principal yachting and boating centres in Northern Ireland.

The Mountains of Mourne above form the highest range in Ulster, reaching 2,796 feet in Slieve Donard, County Down.

Glenelly Valley above right is typical of the scenery of County Tyrone, Ireland's most attractive inland county.

A whitewashed cottage nestles among the trees of County Fermanagh left.

West of Garrison, Lough Melvin below provides good salmon and trout fishing in a breathtakingly beautiful landscape. Equally picturesque is Upper Lough Erne right, one of two extensive lakes in County Fermanagh, both of which have many islands.

It was scenery such as this at Derry, Benevenagh *left, which inspired the traditional Irish melody, the 'Derry Air', said to have been composed in the 6th century by an itinerant Irish harpist.*

Londonderry above, finely situated on the River Foyle, is an ancient and historic town which dates from the foundation of a monastery by St. Colmcille (Columba) in the year 546. Today the city is also an important port, naval base and garrison town. The scene in Derry below was doubtless also familiar to the saint.

Downhill Strand above right is a peaceful seaside resort where once lived the Bishop of Derry and Earl of Bristol, Frederick Harvey.

Ness Wood right is best known for its proximity to Burntollet, whose river is set in a magnificent nature trail.

Dunluce Castle *centre right is an impressive ruin perched on a seagirt rock. It is believed to have been built c.1300 by Richard de Burgh, Earl of Ulster.*

Carrickfergus Castle *above was named after Fergus, the first King of Scotland, who was drowned near here. It is historically associated with the de Courcy's and the de Lucy's and other Norman knights and was held for a while by Robert Bruce.*

The wishing arch *right is one of the most spectacular rock formations of the Antrim coast below.*

County Antrim's White Rocks *left are vivid with sea pinks.*

Ballintoy *below right is a small village which derives its chief interest from the well-known Carrick-a-rede, the passage of the salmon, separated from the mainland by a deep chasm 60 feet wide, through which the sea rushes tumultuously.*

The beautiful cascading waterfall *below is in Glenoe, a tiny, picturesque village in County Antrim.*